D0461642

XTREME JOBS

ASTRONAUT

BY S.L. HAMILTON

A&D Xtreme
An imprint of Abdo Publishing | www.abdopublishing.com

Visit us at
www.abdopublishing.com

Published by Abdo Publishing Company, a division of ABDO, PO Box 398166, Minneapolis, Minnesota 55439. Copyright ©2016 by Abdo Consulting Group, Inc. International copyrights reserved in all countries. No part of this book may be reproduced in any form without written permission from the publisher. A&D Xtreme™ is a trademark and logo of Abdo Publishing Company.

Printed in the United States of America, North Mankato, Minnesota.
052015
092015

Editor: John Hamilton
Graphic Design: Sue Hamilton
Cover Design: Sue Hamilton
Cover Photo: NASA
Interior Photos: All photos courtesy of NASA, except:
pg 7 (top)-Science Source; pg 25 (top)-The Boeing Company.

Websites
To learn more about Xtreme Jobs, visit booklinks.abdopublishing.com. These links are routinely monitored and updated to provide the most current information available.

Library of Congress Control Number: 2015930951

Cataloging-in-Publication Data

Hamilton, S.L.
 Astronaut / S.L Hamilton.
   p. cm. -- (Xtreme jobs)
 ISBN 978-1-62403-756-6
 1. Astronauts--Juvenile literature.   I. Title.
 629.45--dc23

                                    2015930951

CONTENTS

Astronaut

Astronauts rocket to work at speeds of more than 24,200 miles per hour (38,946 kph). They work more than 40 hours a week. They go on missions that last 3, 6, or even 12 months.

Astronaut Barry Wilmore works outside the International Space Station on February 21, 2015.

Astronauts must be smart, strong, fearless, and patient. Mission training may last up to three years. They must be able to handle stressful and dangerous tasks. They must be willing to die for their job.

XTREME FACT – In 2013, more than 6,100 astronaut candidates (ASCANs) applied to NASA. Eight were accepted.

HISTORY

The first United States astronauts were the "Mercury Seven." They were chosen in April 1959 by the National Aeronautics and Space Administration (NASA). The first American to fly in space was Alan Shepard on May 5, 1961.

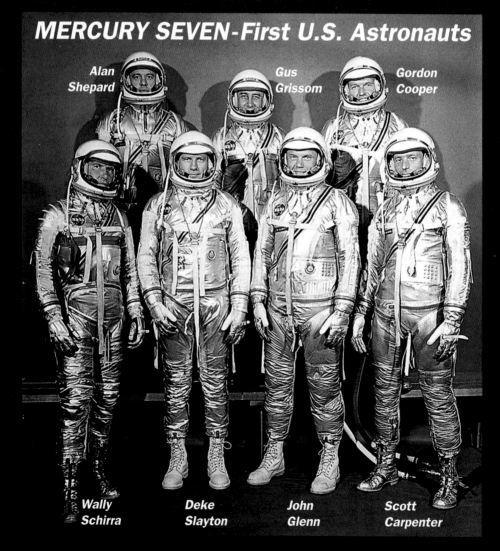

MERCURY SEVEN-First U.S. Astronauts

Alan Shepard

Gus Grissom

Gordon Cooper

Wally Schirra

Deke Slayton

John Glenn

Scott Carpenter

Russian cosmonaut Yuri Gagarin was the first man in space on April 12, 1961. He orbited the Earth in his Vostok 1 spacecraft.

The first men to set foot on the Moon were Neil Armstrong and Buzz Aldrin on July 20, 1969.

From 1959 to 2013, there have been only 330 United States astronauts. They worked for NASA's Mercury, Gemini, Apollo, Space Shuttle, and International Space Station programs. As of 2014, there are 43 active astronauts and 8 astronauts-in-training.

EDUCATION

A college degree in engineering, math, or science is needed to become an astronaut. Candidates must work in their field for at least 3 years or get 1,000 hours of jet aircraft piloting experience. Many future astronauts start out in the U.S. Air Force, Army, Marines, Navy, or Coast Guard.

XTREME FACT – Astronauts must pass a space flight physical. They must have excellent eyesight. They can be no shorter than 5'2" (157 cm) and no taller than 6'3" (190 cm). NASA requires astronauts to learn Russian. It is helpful to know other languages.

TRAINING

Astronauts must learn what it's like to live and work in space. Training takes place at the Johnson Space Center in Houston, Texas. At the Space Vehicle Mockup Facility, astronauts learn how to move in space. They wear a spacesuit and train for extravehicular activities (EVAs), such as spacewalks.

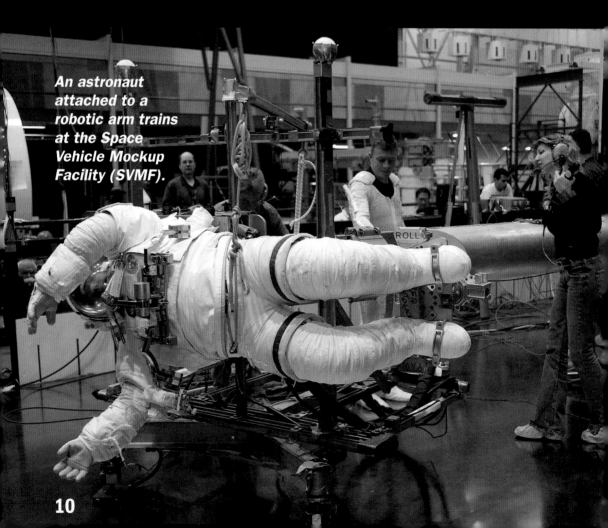

An astronaut attached to a robotic arm trains at the Space Vehicle Mockup Facility (SVMF).

Astronauts train with divers at the Neutral Buoyancy Laboratory. The NBL's pool holds 6.2 million gallons (23.5 million liters) of water.

Johnson Space Center's Neutral Buoyancy Laboratory has the largest indoor pool in the world. It contains full-size models of parts of the International Space Station (ISS). The water environment simulates zero gravity. Astronauts train underwater for more than 100 hours.

INTERNATIONAL SPACE STATION

Astronauts travel 220 miles (354 km) over the Earth to the International Space Station. The first section of the orbiting space lab was launched November 20, 1998. Today, the ISS is as big as a football field.

XTREME FACT – Every person born after November 2, 2000, has lived while an American astronaut orbited above them in the ISS.

One important ISS mission is to find out what happens to humans living in zero gravity. Scientists study the effects of long-term space life on an astronaut's bones, muscles, and heart. NASA will use this information to plan future deep space explorations.

Scott Kelly trains inside a mockup of a Russian Soyuz capsule.

Astronaut Scott Kelly began a 1-year mission aboard the ISS in March 2015. Scott Kelly has an identical twin, former astronaut Mark Kelly. NASA will study the effects of long-term space life by comparing the space twin with the ground twin.

COMMANDER

The job of commander is similar to being the captain of a ship. They give orders. They are responsible for crew safety and other issues affecting the mission. To be chosen commander, astronauts must have flown on previous space missions. They must also be experienced jet aircraft pilots.

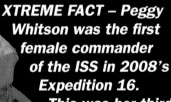

XTREME FACT – Peggy Whitson was the first female commander of the ISS in 2008's Expedition 16. This was her third mission aboard the ISS. To date, she has spent more than 376 days in space.

Commander Steve Swanson (left) takes a portrait with crew members aboard the ISS in 2014.

Commanders work
on everything
from robotics and
lab experiments
to spacewalks.
They have a basic
understanding of
all the other team
members's projects.
Commanders are
also responsible for
maintaining food
and supplies on the
space station.

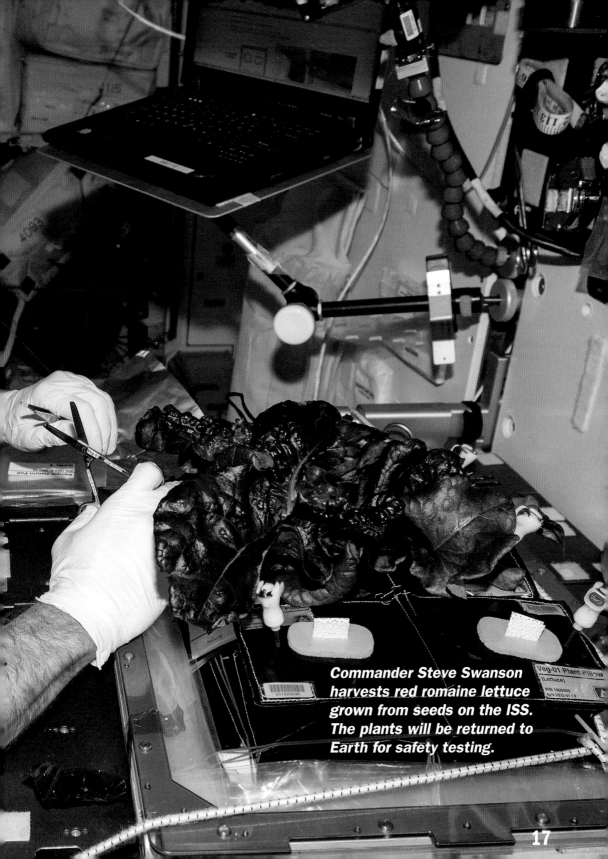

Commander Steve Swanson harvests red romaine lettuce grown from seeds on the ISS. The plants will be returned to Earth for safety testing.

FLIGHT ENGINEER

A flight engineer is a jack-of-all-trades. He or she may work as an engineer, scientist, plumber, cook, or repairman.

Expedition 42's flight engineer, Terry Virts, works from the International Space Station's windowed Cupola in December 2014.

Mullion Pnl
Win5/Win6

B

5

Scratch Pane Win 6

R Lwr Pnl 6

G

H

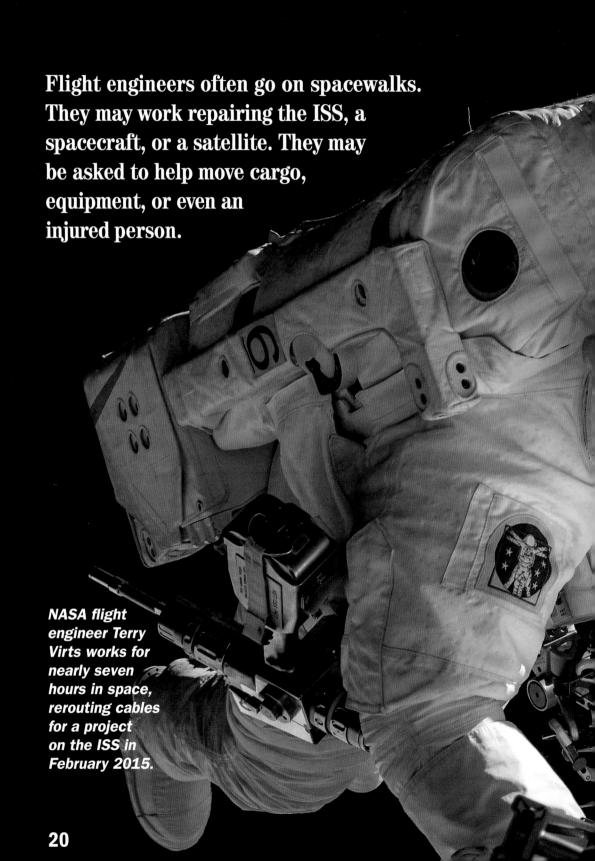

Flight engineers often go on spacewalks. They may work repairing the ISS, a spacecraft, or a satellite. They may be asked to help move cargo, equipment, or even an injured person.

NASA flight engineer Terry Virts works for nearly seven hours in space, rerouting cables for a project on the ISS in February 2015.

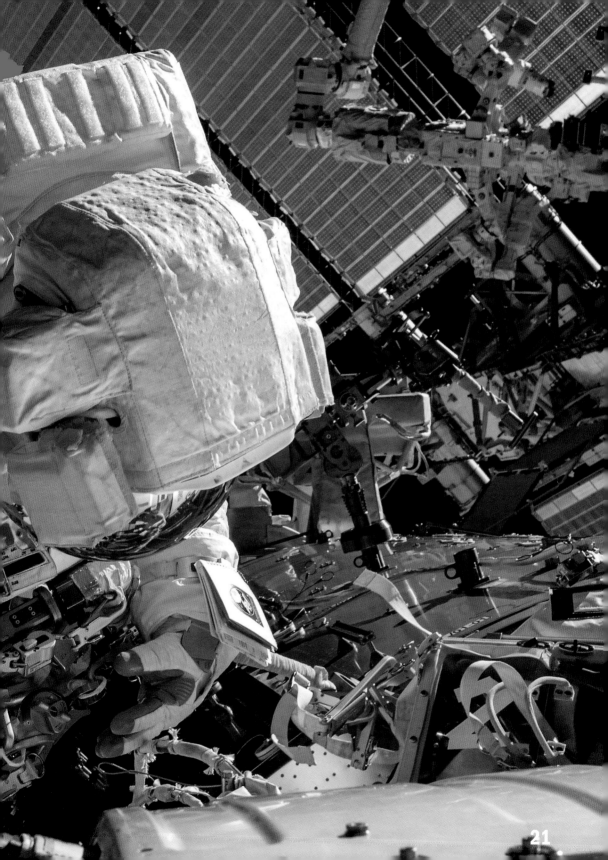

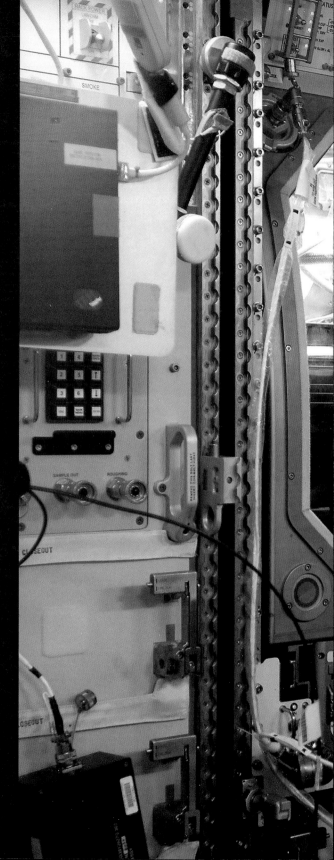

SCIENCE OFFICER

Science officers work on ISS lab projects. They perform experiments in zero gravity that would be impossible to do on Earth. Flight engineers or even commanders may also be science officers.

XTREME FACT– The first ISS science officer was Peggy Whitson. Her degree in biochemistry allowed her to research the changes that occur in living organisms in zero gravity.

Science Officer and Commander Michael Foale works on the ISS's Microgravity Science Glovebox. The MSG is designed with a large window and built-in gloves to allow astronauts to work on experiments in a sealed environment.

COMMERCIAL CREW ASTRONAUTS

Commercial crew astronauts are not employed by NASA. Private companies such as Boeing and SpaceX are building their own spacecraft and training their own crews. NASA will pay these commercial crews to transport astronauts and supplies to the International Space Station.

Commander Chris Hadfield watches from the ISS's Cupola as an unmanned SpaceX Dragon craft prepares to return to Earth after delivering supplies to the space station in 2013.

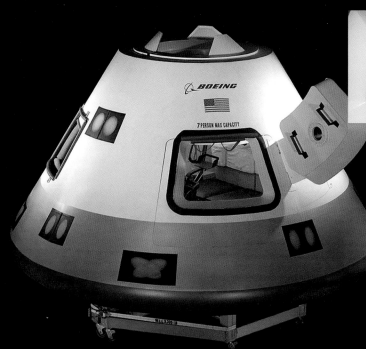

Boeing's CST-100 spacecraft (left) and interior view (above).

SpaceX's Dragon V2 spacecraft.

DEEP SPACE EXPLORATION

The newest NASA vehicle is the Orion Multi-Purpose Crew Vehicle (MPCV). It is designed to carry astronauts farther than any human has ever gone. NASA hopes to send astronauts aboard Orion to an asteroid by 2025.

An illustration of the Orion Multi-Purpose Crew Vehicle (black) attached to a Delta IV upper stage rocket.

An illustration of a manned expedition to Mars.

NASA wants to send astronauts to Mars by the 2030s. Astronauts on the ISS are testing technologies and communications systems to make deep space exploration a reality.

Robotic rovers on Mars have been sending back data for years. Scientists use this information to understand how to keep future explorers safe. Of greatest concern is the radiation astronauts will be subjected to over a three-year Mars mission. Protecting the astronauts is vital.

JOB FACTS

Most astronauts are between the ages of 26 and 46. As of 2015, an astronaut may earn from $66,000 up to $144,000 per year. Astronauts know their work is dangerous, but none would give up the chance to work in space.

XTREME FACT– While no American astronauts have died while "in" space, more than 20 have given their lives training for a mission, or during lift-off or re-entry.

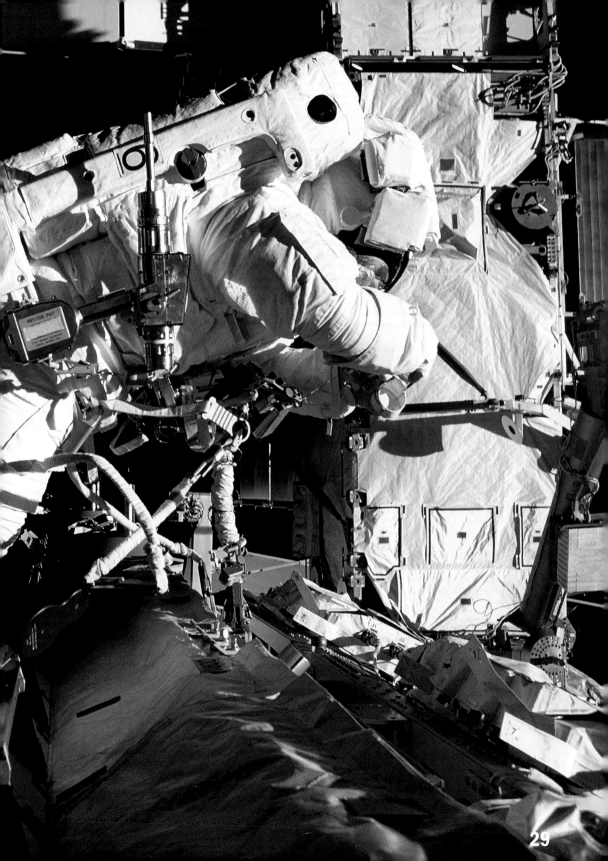

GLOSSARY

APOLLO SPACE PROGRAM
An American space exploration program that ran from 1963 to 1972. Run by NASA, the program's goal was to land astronauts on the Moon and return them safely to Earth. The first Moon landing was achieved by *Apollo 11* on July 20, 1969.

EXTRAVEHICULAR ACTIVITY (EVA)
An EVA is any activity for which an astronaut must go outside the protected environment in which they live while in space. A spacewalk is an EVA.

INTERNATIONAL SPACE STATION (ISS)
An Earth-orbiting space station designed by NASA, the European Space Agency, the Russian Federal Space Agency, the Japan Aerospace Exploration Agency, and the Canadian Space Agency, as well as other countries around the world. The ISS allows astronauts and scientists to live and work in space. Construction of the ISS began in orbit in 1998.

NATIONAL AERONAUTICS AND SPACE ADMINISTRATION (NASA)
A U.S. government agency started in 1958. NASA's goals include space exploration, as well as increasing people's understanding of Earth, our solar system, and the universe. One major NASA facility is the Johnson Space Center in Houston, Texas.

SATELLITE

A mechanical device placed in orbit around the Earth, the Moon, or other planets, designed to send communication signals and/or information back to Earth. A satellite may also refer to a celestial object (such as a moon) that revolves around a planet.

SPACE SHUTTLE

America's first reusable space vehicle. NASA developed five different orbiters: *Columbia, Challenger, Atlantis, Discovery,* and *Endeavour.* The final space shuttle mission (STS-135) was flown on *Atlantis* in July 2011.

ZERO GRAVITY

Weightlessness. An environment, such as space, where people and objects appear to float. The effects of zero gravity may also be felt briefly on Earth. For example, when a person reaches the top of a hill on a fast-moving roller coaster, their body may be lifted out their seat for a few seconds. The person experiences weightlessness.

INDEX

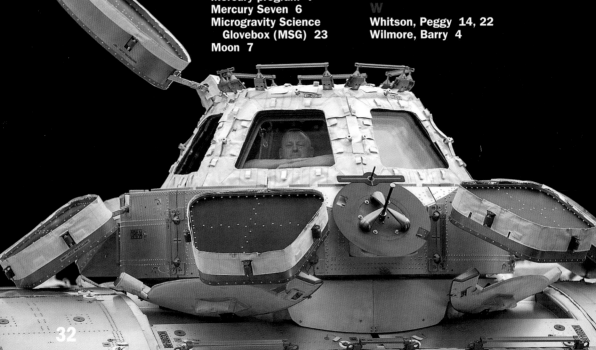